SCARY MOVIE

PETER MILLETT
ANTHEA EDWARDS

GONE with the RAIN

A Very Scary M

NELSON CENGAGE Learning

Australia • Brazil • Japan • Korea • Mexico • Singapore • Spain • United Kingdom • United States

Scary Movie

Fast Forward
Orange Level 16

Text: Peter Millett
Illustrations: Anthea Edwards
Editor: Johanna Rohan
Design: Mandi Cole
Series design: James Lowe
Production controller: Seona Galbally
Audio recordings: Juliet Hill, Picture Start
Spoken by: Matthew King and Abbe Holmes
Reprint: Jennifer Foo

ISBN 978 0 17 012613 7
ISBN 978 0 17 012609 0 (set)

Cengage Learning Australia
Level 7, 80 Dorcas Street
South Melbourne, Victoria Australia 3205
Phone: 1300 790 853

Cengage Learning New Zealand
Unit 4B Rosedale Office Park
331 Rosedale Road, Albany, North Shore NZ 0632
Phone: 0800 449 725

For learning solutions, visit **cengage.com.au**

Printed in Australia by Ligare Pty Ltd
7 8 9 10 11 12 13 20 19 18 17 16

Evaluated in independent research by staff from the Department of Language, Literacy and Arts Education at the University of Melbourne.

SCARY MOVIE

PETER MILLETT
ANTHEA EDWARDS

Contents

Chapter 1

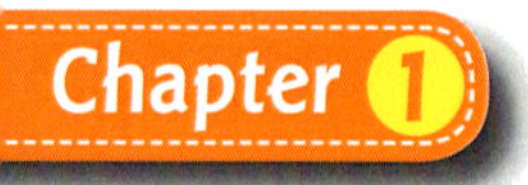

Gary

Mr and Mrs Smith handed the girls
their phone number
in case they needed to call.
"Thanks for baby-sitting tonight,"
said Mrs Smith.
"We're so grateful.
We haven't been out for dinner
in a long time."

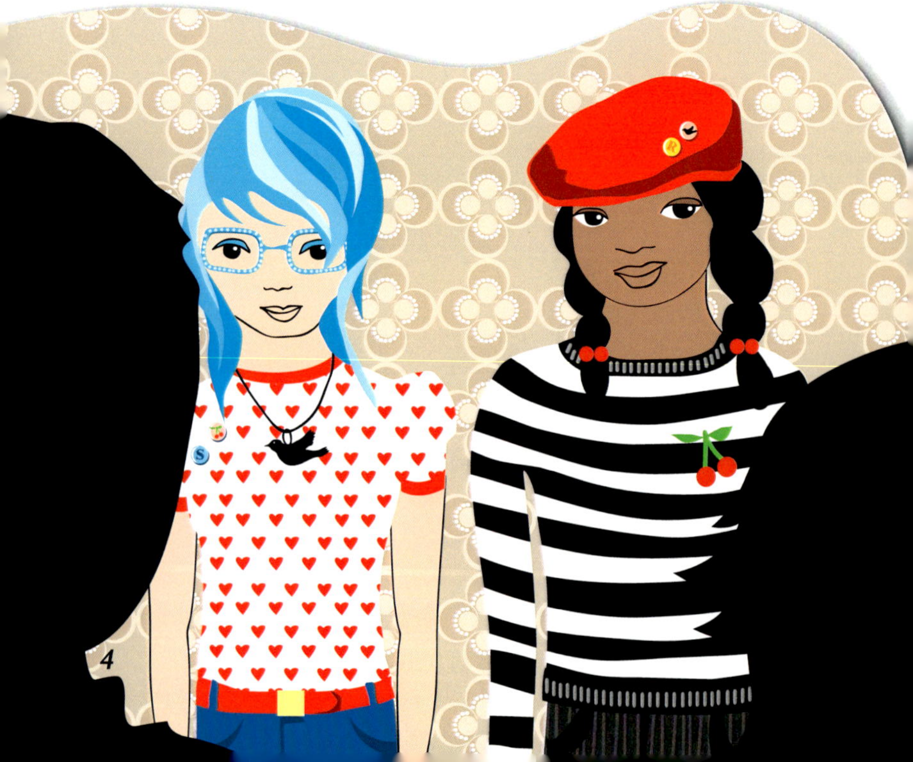

Mr Smith smiled.
"There's some pizza on the bench,
and a movie for you to watch."

"Great!" said Rebecca.

"Thanks," said Simone.

Mr and Mrs Smith put on their coats
and got ready to leave.

Mr Smith tapped the top of a glass cage on his way out.
"Don't worry about Gary,"
he laughed.
"He looks a little scary,
but he wouldn't hurt a fly!"

Mr and Mrs Smith then left for dinner.

"Who's Gary?" asked Rebecca.

Simone walked over to the glass cage and looked inside.
But, she couldn't see anything.
"I don't know what Mr Smith was talking about," Simone said.

GONE with the RAIN
A Very Scary Movie

Rebecca put on the DVD.
"What's the movie?" asked Simone.

"It's called *Gone with the Rain*."

"I hope it isn't scary," said Simone.
"I hate scary movies ..."

Simone and Rebecca sat down on the couch and waited for the movie to start.

Chapter 2

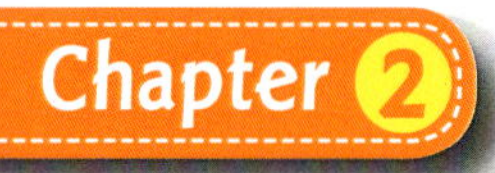

Do Something!

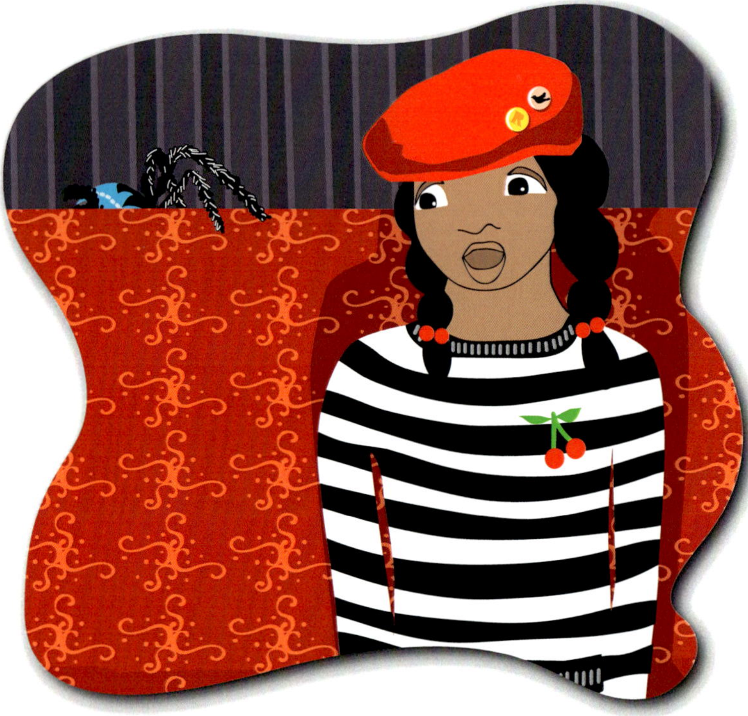

Rebecca reached for the remote control to turn up the sound.
Suddenly, she saw three long, hairy legs curling up over the couch.
"Argh!" she screamed and jumped back.

Simone turned around.
Her eyes were as big as basketballs.
A huge spider was crawling over
the back of the couch.

"Argh!" she gasped.

Rebecca dropped the remote control.
Simone wriggled back.

"Do something! Do something!"
Simone yelled.
Every time Simone wriggled,
the spider moved closer.
"Keep still," whispered Rebecca.

Simone stopped wriggling
and tried to breathe slowly.
"What are we going to do?"
she asked.

"Nothing," whispered Rebecca.
"If we sit still, then maybe the spider
will go away."

Chapter 3

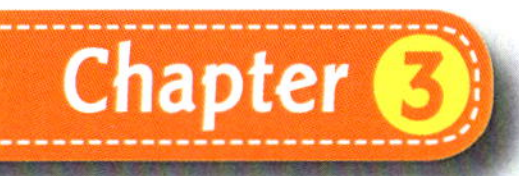

Sitting Still

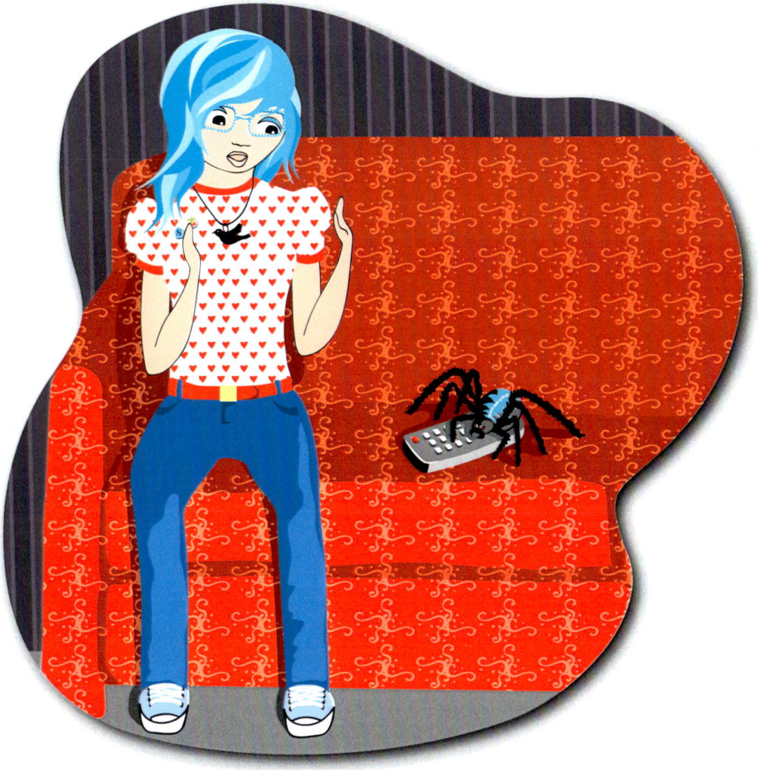

Suddenly, the spider crawled
across the seat,
and jumped on top of the
remote control.
Simone held up her hands in fear.

The two girls sat silently
while the movie kept playing.
They sat still for nearly two hours,
waiting for the spider to crawl away.

The spider didn't move an inch. It just sat there on top of the remote control.

Chapter 4

Friendly Gary

"I can't take this any longer," whispered Simone. "I'm going to make a run for it!"

"No, don't!" cried Rebecca.

Suddenly, the door opened.
Mr and Mrs Smith were back
from dinner.
"It's as quiet as a library in here,"
smiled Mr Smith.
He stared at the spider sitting between
the girls.

"Gary!" yelled Mr Smith.
He turned to Mrs Smith.
"Gary has escaped from his cage again!
Can you believe it?"

"No way!" cried Mrs Smith.
"That's the second time this month."

Mr Smith raced over
and scooped up the spider
in his hands.
Then, he gave him a kiss,
and showed him to the girls.
"See how friendly Gary is?"
he said.
"He wouldn't hurt a fly!"

Simone and Rebecca looked at each other.

Mr Smith carefully placed Gary back into his cage.
"So, girls, what did you think of the movie?" he asked.
"I hope it wasn't too scary for you ..."